OUR BODY

Respiratory System

Cheryl Jakab

Smart Apple Media

This edition first published in 2006 in the United States of America by Smart Apple Media.

Smart Apple Media
2140 Howard Drive West
North Mankato
Minnesota 56003

First published in 2006 by
MACMILLAN EDUCATION AUSTRALIA PTY LTD
627 Chapel Street, South Yarra, Australia 3141

Visit our Web site at www.macmillan.com.au

Associated companies and representatives throughout the world.

Library of Congress Cataloging-in-Publication Data

Jakab, Cheryl.
    The respiratory system / by Cheryl Jakab.
    p. cm. — (Our body)
    Includes index.
    ISBN-13: 978-1-58340-736-3
    1. Respiratory organs—Juvenile literature. 2. Respiration—Juvenile literature. I. Title.

QP121.J35 2006
612.2'1—dc22   2005056798

Edited by Ruth Jelley
Text and cover design by Peter Shaw
Illustrations by Guy Holt, Jeff Lang (p. 4 (bottom), pp. 5–6),
    and Ann Likhovetsky (p. 30)
Photo research by Legend Images

Printed in USA

Acknowledgments

The author and the publisher are grateful to the following for permission to reproduce copyright material:

Front cover photograph: Light micrograph of a section through human lung tissue, showing alveoli, courtesy of Photolibrary/Astrid & Hanns-Frieder Michler/Science Photo Library. Front cover illustration by Jeff Lang.

Laurent H. Americain-SBIP/Auscape International, p. 26; The DW Stock Picture Library, pp. 20, 22; © Peter E. Smith, Natural Sciences Image Library, p. 23; Photolibrary/Index Stock Imagery, p. 28; Photolibrary/Science Photo Library, pp. 9, 16, 19, 25, 29.

While every care has been taken to trace and acknowledge copyright, the publisher tenders their apologies for any accidental infringement where copyright has proved untraceable. Where the attempt has been unsuccessful, the publisher welcomes information that would redress the situation.

Contents

Glossary words
When a word is printed in **bold**,
you can look up its meaning
in the Glossary on page 31.

Amazing body structures

The human body is an amazing living thing. The structures of the body are divided into systems. Each system is made up of **cells**. Huge numbers of cells make up the **tissues** of the body systems. Each system performs a different, vital function. This series looks at six of the systems in the most familiar living thing to you—your body.

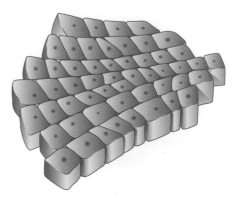

Cells make up tissues of the body systems.

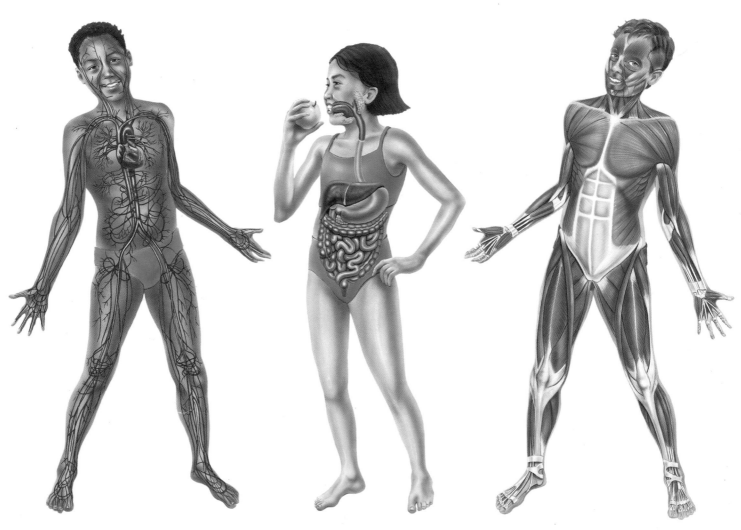

circulatory system   digestive system   muscular system

The respiratory system

The respiratory system delivers oxygen to the blood and removes carbon dioxide from the blood. How much do you know about your respiratory system?

- Do you know how your lungs work?
- What does oxygen do for your body?
- How does your body remove carbon dioxide?
- Do you know what happens in an asthma attack?

This book looks at the human respiratory system to answer these questions and more.

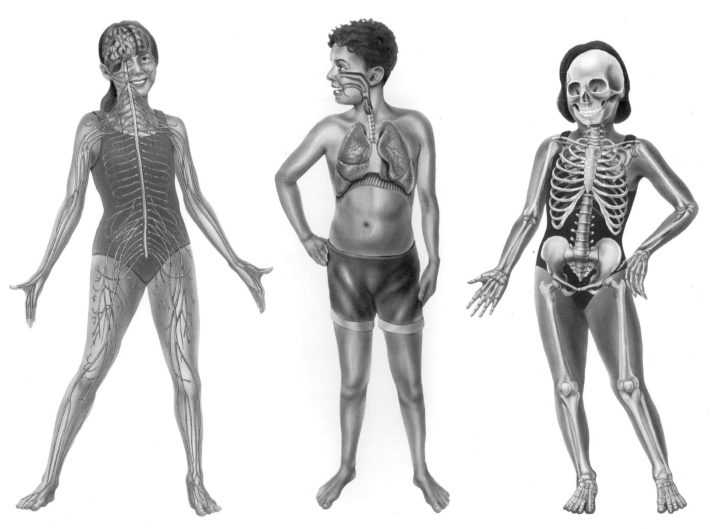

nervous system

respiratory system

skeletal system

Parts of the respiratory system

The respiratory system is a complex network in the head and chest. It is made up of:

- the air passages, from the nose down the throat to the chest
- the lungs, which take up most of the space in the chest cavity
- the muscles in the chest and the **diaphragm**

You and your lungs

Although your lungs work constantly, most of the time you do not even think about them. You become very aware of your breathing when you get out of breath during exercise, or if you are under water.

nose
nasal cavity
throat
trachea
right bronchus
left bronchus
right lung
left lung
diaphragm

FASCINATING FACT
Being able to speak depends on air from the lungs passing over small folds in the throat called vocal cords.

Bronchial tree

The system of respiratory passageways is called the "bronchial tree" because it branches out like an upside down tree. The airways, starting at the nose and mouth, divide into branches called **bronchi**. As they enter the lungs they divide into finer and finer air passages.

Each lung is made up of smaller units called lobes. Each lobe is served by a different branch of the bronchial tree. The right lung has three lobes while the left lung has only two. This is to allow space for the heart.

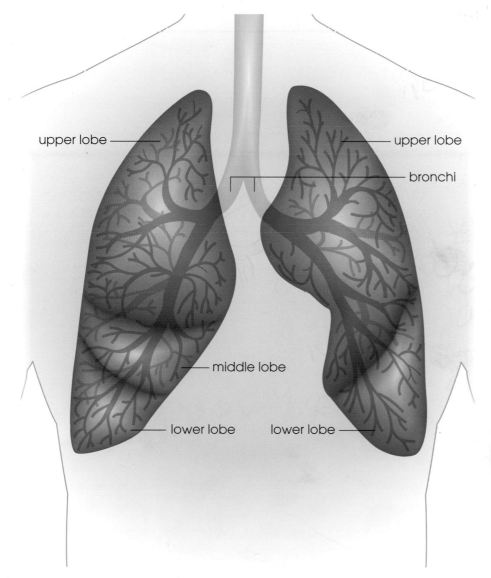

upper lobe

upper lobe

bronchi

middle lobe

lower lobe

lower lobe

Bronchi carry air in and out of the lungs.

TRY THIS

Slow breathing

Slow breathing relaxes the body.

Sit with your eyes closed and breathe in deeply and slowly through your nose. Breathe out slowly through your mouth.

Can you feel your lungs expand and contract with each breath?

You should feel yourself relax after just a few breaths.

Parts of the lungs

Many different parts make up the structure of the lungs. Each lung is covered by a thin layer like a bag, called the pleural **membrane**.

Inside the lungs, **bronchioles** branch off from the bronchi, to reach every part of the lungs. Deep within the lungs, the bronchioles end in tiny air sacs, called **alveoli** (say al-vee-ol-ee), which look like bunches of grapes. The bronchioles are like the stalks from which the grapes hang. There are about 30,000 alveoli in each lung.

The passageways of the lungs are lined with cells that produce **mucus**. This keeps them moist.

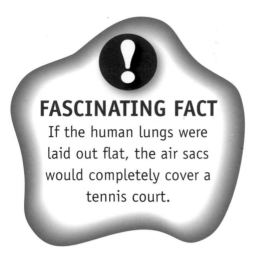

FASCINATING FACT
If the human lungs were laid out flat, the air sacs would completely cover a tennis court.

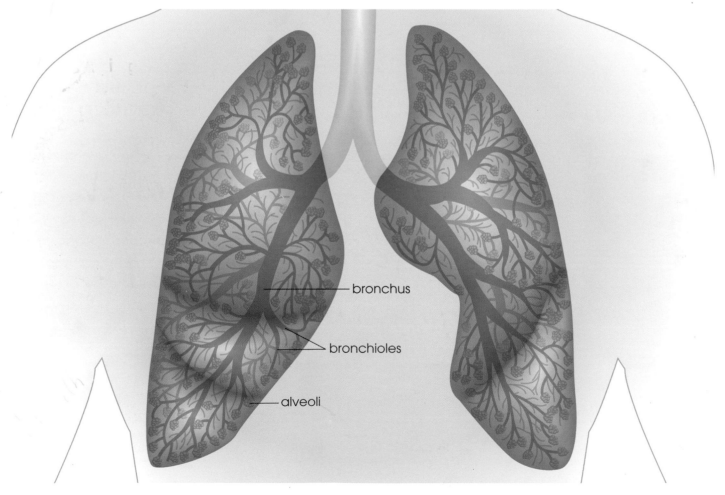

bronchus

bronchioles

alveoli

The lungs fill up most of the chest cavity.

Alveoli

Alveoli make up the bulk of the lung tissue. A single alveolus is very tiny. About 400 of them would fit in 0.2 square inch (1 sq cm). The walls of the alveoli are elastic so they can expand and contract as air moves in and out of them. Alveoli occur in bunches within an alveolar sac. The walls of the alveoli have a very rich network of blood vessels traveling through them.

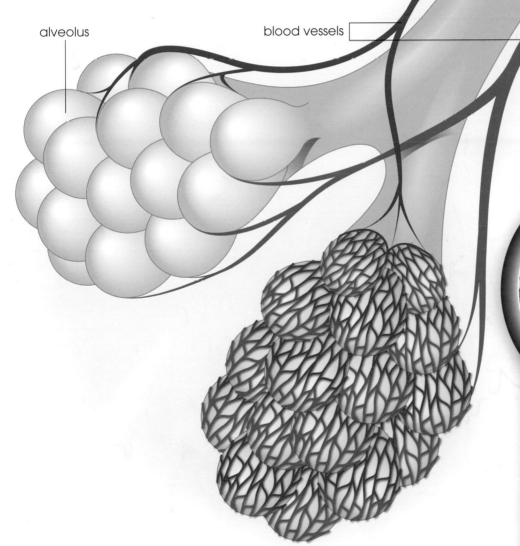

alveolus

blood vessels

Lung tissue UNDER THE MICROSCOPE

Lung tissue is made up of large amounts of empty space created by the alveoli. The alveoli walls are very thin. The thinnest wall is just one cell thick.

Alveoli are tiny air sacs at the ends of the bronchioles inside the lungs.

The nose and mouth

The nose and mouth are the entrances to a large space in the head. The mouth connects to the respiratory passageway in the back of the throat. The nostrils and nasal cavity are lined with a sticky membrane that produces mucus to keep them moist. There are tiny hairs, called **cilia**, on the surface of this membrane which act as filters to trap dust and other particles from the air.

The cilia have receptors which detect chemicals (smells) in the air. There are over 10,000,000 smell receptors which can detect about 10,000 smells.

!

FASCINATING FACT
A sneeze is a sudden movement of air out of the nose. The air forced out moves at more than 98 miles (160 km) per hour.

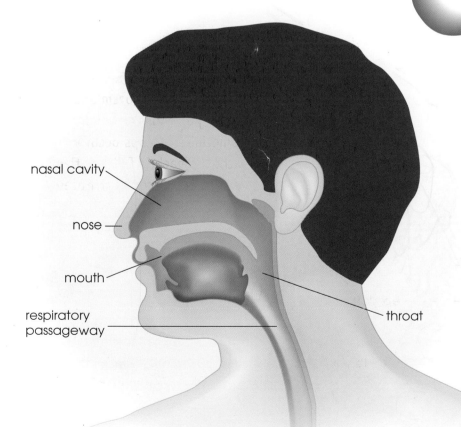

nasal cavity

nose

mouth

respiratory passageway

throat

Air enters the respiratory system through the nose and mouth.

10

Pharynx

The respiratory passage in the throat, the **pharynx**, is made up of three parts. The top part behind the nose only allows air to pass through it. Both air and food pass through the lower parts.

The epiglottis

The epiglottis is small flap of elastic **cartilage** that closes off the airway when food is swallowed. It controls the two passageways in the lower pharynx which lead to either the lungs or the stomach and prevents food entering the lungs.

The larynx

The larynx, which sits below the epiglottis, is where the voice is generated. It consists of folds in the surface of the throat, which vibrate to create sound when air passes over them.

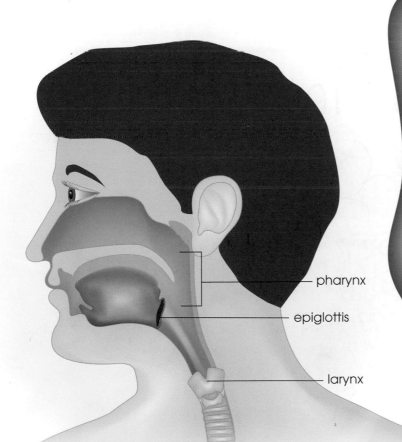

pharynx

epiglottis

larynx

HEALTH TIP
Hiccups
Hiccups occur when the epiglottis muscles go into spasm and the flap jumps back and forth. Sometimes hiccups occur when the stomach is full and the diaphragm becomes irritated.

Tip: To stop hiccups, hold your breath and keep the diaphragm still.

Parts of the throat play an important role in the respiratory system.

The trachea and bronchi

The **trachea**, also known as the windpipe, is the large tube that runs down the throat below the pharynx. It branches into the two primary bronchi in the middle of the chest.

Trachea

The trachea is supported by large C-shaped rings of cartilage. These prevent the trachea from collapsing. Stretchy connective tissue and muscle connect the cartilage rings to each other. This makes the trachea flexible, so it can bend with the body.

Bronchi

The two primary bronchi each go to a different lung. The right bronchus leads to the right lung and the left bronchus leads to the left lung. The bronchi also have cartilage rings for support.

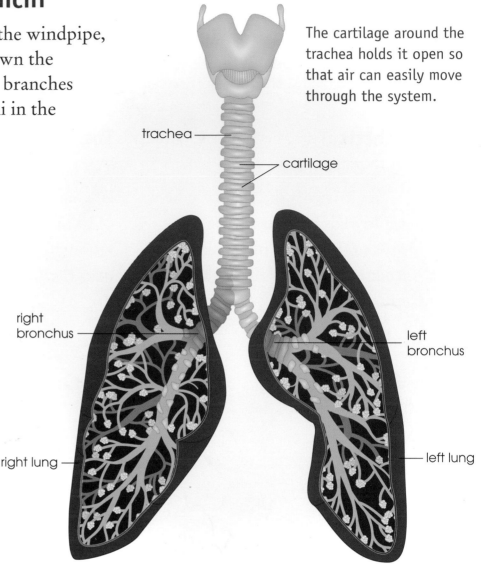

The cartilage around the trachea holds it open so that air can easily move through the system.

trachea

cartilage

right bronchus

left bronchus

right lung

left lung

TRY THIS

Rings of cartilage

Hold your head high and tilt it back slightly to stretch the neck. Gently feel down the front of the neck with two fingers. The hard bands you can feel are rings of cartilage around the trachea.

12

Inside the lungs

Inside the lungs, the primary bronchi branch out into secondary bronchi. These smaller branches are supported by muscle and cartilage. As the airways continue to branch out within the lungs, they become narrower and narrower. The smallest airways, the respiratory bronchioles, do not have any muscle or cartilage supporting them.

Around the lungs

There are 12 pairs of ribs which provide protection for the lungs and the heart. Together with the upper spine, the ribs create a cage around the chest. The breastbone, or sternum, is a piece of cartilage in the middle of the chest that provides added protection. The first ten pairs of ribs are connected to the sternum by flexible cartilage. The last two pairs of ribs are much shorter and do not wrap around the front of the body.

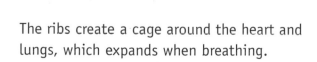

sternum

heart

right lung

left lung

The ribs create a cage around the heart and lungs, which expands when breathing.

Breathing

Breathing moves air in and out of the lungs. Inside the alveoli, gases are transferred to and from the blood. This exchange is called **respiration**.

External and internal respiration

External respiration is the exchange of gases in the lungs. Oxygen is transferred into the blood and carbon dioxide is transferred out of the blood. Carbon dioxide is then breathed out.

Internal respiration is the exchange of gases in the body's tissues. Oxygen-rich blood travels to all parts of the body to exchange gases with other body tissues. Oxygen passes into the tissues from the blood, and carbon dioxide passes from the tissues into the blood. Blood carrying carbon dioxide then returns to the lungs for external respiration.

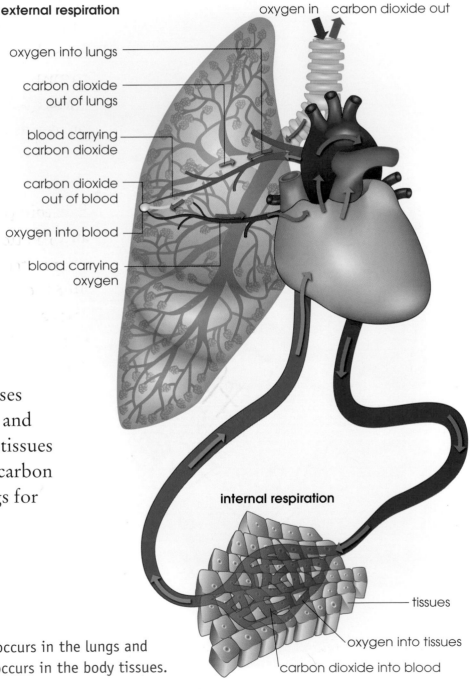

external respiration

oxygen in   carbon dioxide out

oxygen into lungs

carbon dioxide out of lungs

blood carrying carbon dioxide

carbon dioxide out of blood

oxygen into blood

blood carrying oxygen

internal respiration

tissues

oxygen into tissues

carbon dioxide into blood

External respiration occurs in the lungs and internal respiration occurs in the body tissues.

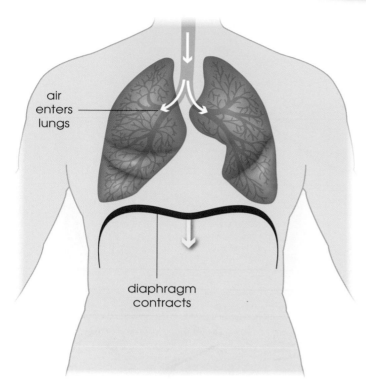

Contraction of the diaphragm increases the size of the chest cavity, allowing air to enter the lungs.

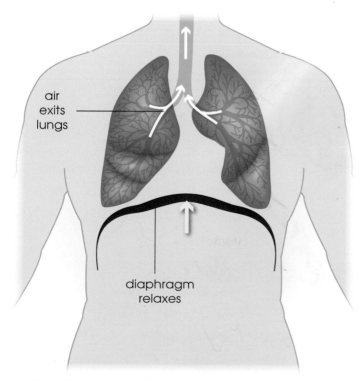

As the diaphragm relaxes, air is pushed out of the lungs.

The action of breathing

The action of breathing is controlled by the diaphragm. During **inhalation** the diaphragm contracts, pulling downwards and enlarging the chest. During **exhalation** the diaphragm relaxes, making the chest cavity smaller. The increase in the size of the chest cavity reduces the pressure inside the lungs. Air then moves inwards towards the lungs. As the pressure in the chest cavity rises, the air in the lungs flows outwards.

Controlling breathing

Breathing is normally controlled by automatic signals from the brain. The respiratory center in the brain controls the muscles involved in breathing. Breathing can be stopped for a short while, but not for long because the body tissues need a constant supply of oxygen.

FASCINATING FACT
Not all the air that is breathed in is used by the body. Some of the air does not reach the lungs at all. It only gets as far as the nose, trachea, or bronchi.

Gas exchange

Gas exchange takes place in the smallest blood vessels, the capillaries. In the lungs, oxygen moves across the membranes of the alveoli and capillaries to the blood where there is a low concentration of oxygen. At the same time, carbon dioxide passes from the blood into the alveoli. In the body tissue, oxygen from the blood passes to the tissues and carbon dioxide moves into the blood.

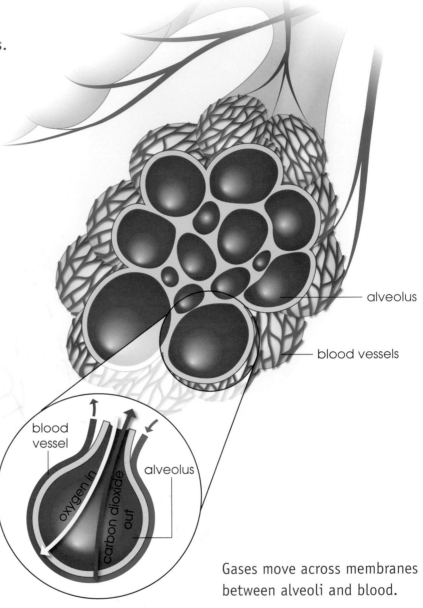

alveolus

blood vessels

blood vessel

oxygen in

carbon dioxide out

alveolus

Gases move across membranes between alveoli and blood.

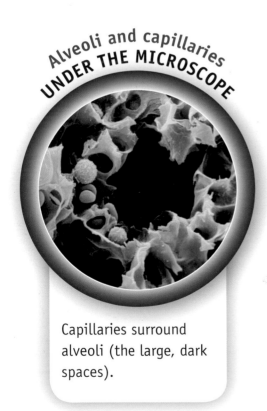

Alveoli and capillaries
UNDER THE MICROSCOPE

Capillaries surround alveoli (the large, dark spaces).

Oxygen and waste gases

Body tissues need oxygen to carry out all their activities. Muscles need it for contracting and nerves need it for carrying messages. As these activities occur, waste products, such as carbon dioxide, are produced. Carbon dioxide is removed from the body through the lungs.

Blood in the lungs

The circulation of blood from the heart to the lungs is separate from the circulation to the rest of the body. Inside the lungs, large blood vessels branch into smaller and smaller blood vessels. These blood vessels carry blood to each lobe of the lungs for gas exchange. Blood that lacks oxygen is pumped into the lungs from the heart. The blood picks up oxygen in the lungs. The oxygen-rich blood flows back to the heart to then be pumped to all the tissues of the body.

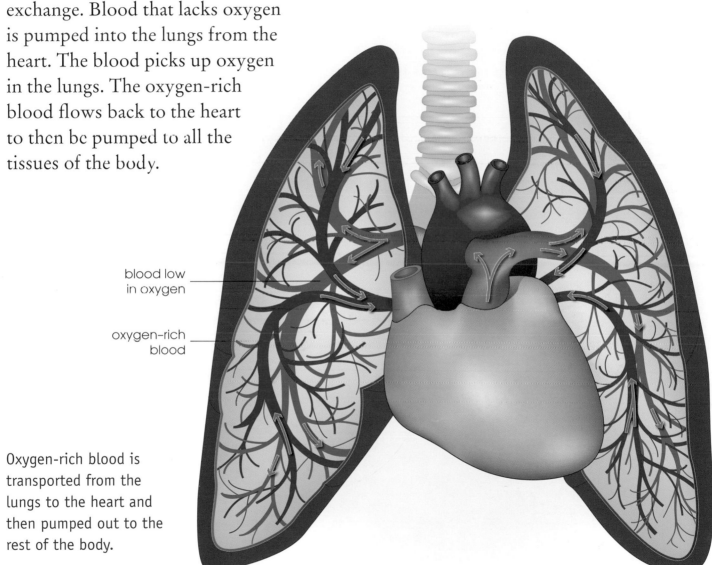

blood low
in oxygen

oxygen-rich
blood

Oxygen-rich blood is transported from the lungs to the heart and then pumped out to the rest of the body.

Oxygen for lung tissue

The lung tissues also need oxygen to function. They have their own oxygen-rich supply of blood. This blood supply flows to the lungs in blood vessels called bronchial arteries.

Changes in the respiratory system

Before birth a developing baby's lungs do not function. The baby gets its oxygen from the mother's body, which also removes carbon dioxide. This occurs through an organ called the placenta. The respiratory system changes suddenly at birth when the baby first breathes for itself.

The lungs at birth

At birth, a baby uses its lungs for the first time, which is a very significant change in the baby's body. The lungs inflate and must provide oxygen to the body within minutes. Before birth, the lungs are kept partially inflated by a substance called surfactant, which is produced by the alveoli. Surfactant creates a tight layer inside the alveoli which holds them open like tight little balloons.

Surfactant holds the alveoli open and prevents them from collapsing so they can fill with air at birth.

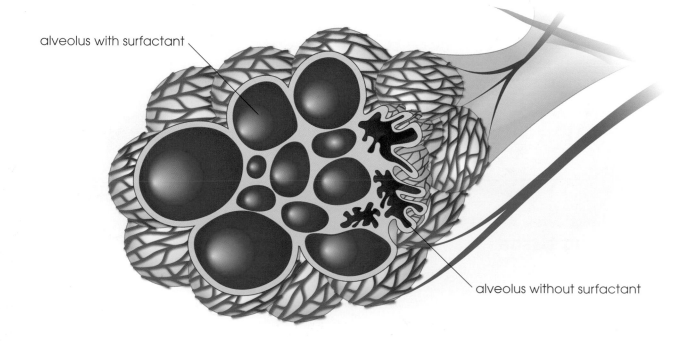

alveolus with surfactant

alveolus without surfactant

Lung growth and capacity

Lung capacity increases as the body grows and the lungs get bigger. Lung capacity for a child aged 3 to 5 years is about 3.5 pints (2 l). This increases to 5.3 pints (3 l) by the time a child reaches 10 years of age. By the age of 15 years, lung capacity reaches about 7 to 8.8 pints (4 to 5 l). Normal lung capacity for an adult is about 10.6 pints (6 l).

Using lung capacity

In normal breathing, only a small part of the total lung capacity is used. Although lung capacity for an adult is about 10.6 pints (6 l), only around 7 pints (4 l) can ever be exhaled. The maximum amount that can be exhaled is known as the vital capacity.

TRY THIS

Vital capacity

Find your vital lung capacity by breathing in as deeply as you can and then blowing into a paper bag. Fill the bag up with as much air as you can blow out in one breath. The volume of the blown-up bag is your vital capacity.

Lung capacity is measured by blowing into a peak flow meter.

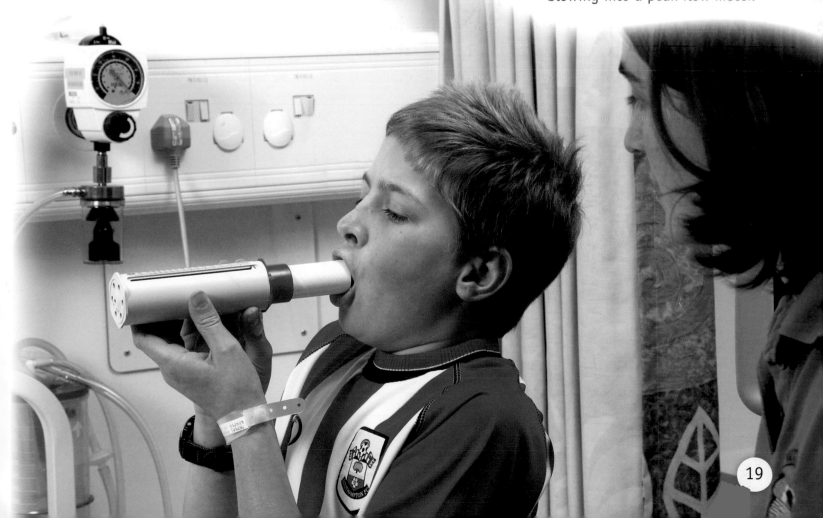

Changes to breathing

Breathing changes as the body's need for oxygen changes.
This occurs without any conscious thought during activities
such as exercising. Both the breathing rate and the depth of
breathing can change.

Breathing rate

The breathing rate is the number of breaths taken per minute.
The resting breathing rate is measured by sitting still and
counting the number of breaths taken in one minute.
The normal resting rate is 12 to 15 breaths per minute.
A normal resting breath consists of about two seconds of
inhaling and about three seconds of exhaling.

The breathing rate
increases when running.

Tidal volume

The amount of air that moves in and out of the lungs is called the tidal volume. Tidal volume can vary as the depth of breathing changes. While resting, the normal tidal volume is about 0.9 pints (0.5 l). In shallow breathing the tidal volume is about 0.4 pints (0.2 l). The tidal volume of a deep breath averages around 1.8 pints (1 l).

Deep breathing

Deep breathing involves taking in large tidal volumes, which are usually less than the total vital capacity. The tidal volume of an athlete who is breathing deeply can be as much as 5.3 pints (3 l).

The small amount of air that stays in the upper airways is about 0.2 pints (0.1 l). This makes up only a small proportion of a very deep breath.

TRY THIS

Shallow breathing

Take five short, shallow breaths in ten seconds.

This very fast puffing makes it difficult to get air deep into the lungs. You can feel that most of the flow of air is in the nose and upper trachea.

Comparing breathing rates

Deep breathing is more effective for delivering a large amount of oxygen to the lungs. Short, shallow breaths deliver less oxygen than when breathing at a normal rate.

Type of breathing	Breaths per minute	Tidal volume per breath	Total air breathed in one minute
fast and shallow	30	0.4 pints	30 x 0.4 pints = 12 pints
normal	20	1.1 pints	20 x 1.1 pints = 22 pints
slow and deep	10	6.4 pints	10 x 6.4 pints = 64 pints

Keeping the respiratory system healthy

The respiratory system needs fresh air and a regular heavy workout to stay healthy.

Exercise and breathing

Exercise that makes the respiratory system work hard helps to develop strong **respiratory muscles**. Deep breathing while exercising also clears the alveoli and helps keep their walls stretched open. Healthy lungs are needed for strenuous exercise, and strenuous exercise also keeps the lungs healthy.

Air pollution

Air pollution can cause a range of breathing difficulties. Living in cities where the air is not always clean is not good for the lungs. Weather forecasts often contain health warnings if air pollution is expected to be high. People with breathing problems need to reduce activity levels on days of high pollution.

(!)

FASCINATING FACT
Humans cannot breathe under water. People can swim below the surface of the water and use a snorkel to breathe. People who go deeper under water need to carry an oxygen tank with them.

Respiratory muscles develop strength with exercises that increase breathing.

Exercising the respiratory muscles

The respiratory muscles get a good workout with deep, strong breathing. Exercising these muscles makes it easier for them to change the pressures in the chest.

Sometimes the diaphragm starts to hurt during exercise. This is what is commonly known as a "stitch." It can be caused by a lack of oxygen supplied to the diaphragm. Taking a few deep breaths gives the diaphragm the chance to refresh itself, and makes the stitch go away.

Recovery rate

A good measure of the health of the respiratory system is how quickly breathing returns to normal after exercising. The faster it returns to normal, the healthier the body systems are, including the respiratory system.

TRY THIS

Test your recovery rate

Record the number of breaths you take in 15 seconds when at rest. Then run for about three minutes. Count and record your breathing rate for each 15 seconds until it returns to your resting rate. How long did it take?

Regular singing practice helps to develop strong respiratory muscles.

Respiratory problems

Respiratory infections and diseases are significant problems for many people.

Upper respiratory tract infections

Infections in the upper respiratory tract range from colds to serious viral infections, such as influenza, or severe bronchitis. Tiny **organisms** in the air we breathe can become lodged in the airways and multiply, causing disease.

HEALTH TIP

Laryngitis and tonsillitis

Laryngitis occurs when the folds of the larynx swell, preventing them from producing sound. Tonsillitis is an infection of the tonsils, which sit at the back of the throat.

Tip: Treat the first signs of a sore throat by gargling with salt mixed with water.

Bronchitis

Bronchitis means "infection of the bronchi." It can be a simple viral infection, or a chronic long-term problem. Long-term bronchitis is often associated with smoking or other pollutants.

Pneumonia

Infection in the lungs is known as pneumonia (say new-mo-nee-ah). This dangerous infection affects the alveoli and causes problems with external respiration.

Tonsillitis and laryngitis can cause a sore throat, and bronchitis and pneumonia cause ongoing coughing.

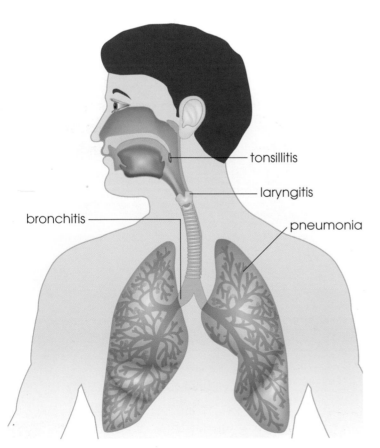

tonsillitis

laryngitis

bronchitis

pneumonia

Lung cancers

Cancer is the growth of abnormal cells. Inhaling chemicals that irritate the lungs can cause cancers. Irritants that are cancer-causing (carcinogenic) include tobacco smoke, coal dust, and asbestos.

Smoking and the lungs

The most common cause of lung cancer is smoking. Tobacco smoke contains over 3,000 chemicals, many of which irritate lung tissue.

Factors that determine the development of cancer include the number of cigarettes a person has smoked, the number of years they have smoked for, and how deeply they inhaled the smoke.

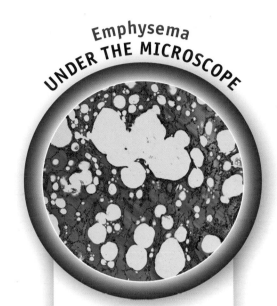

Emphysema
UNDER THE MICROSCOPE

Emphysema (say em-fah-see-mah) occurs in long-term smokers, and causes alveoli to break down. It creates large spaces (white areas) where gas exchange cannot take place.

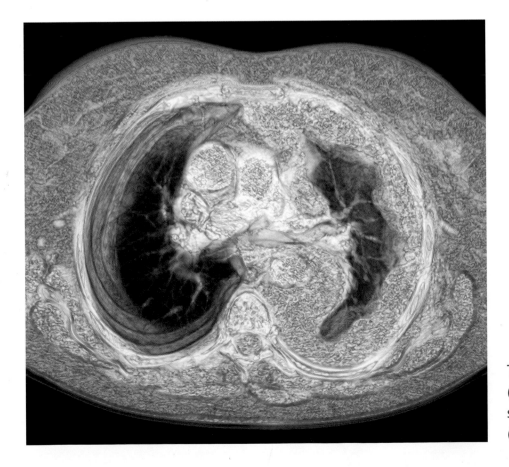

This scan shows cancer (yellow/blue color) surrounding the left lung (on the right of the photo).

Diagnosing respiratory problems

The stethoscope is a useful tool for diagnosing respiratory problems. It allows doctors to listen to the lungs and find out if they are working properly. A range of other medical imaging techniques are also used in diagnosing respiratory problems.

Chest X rays and scans

A chest X ray can show up some abnormalities in lungs. However, X rays may not show the details of the abnormalities, so CT scans are often used to diagnose lung problems. CT scans consist of multiple X rays that are put together using a computer to create a detailed image.

Lobectomy

If part of a lung becomes diseased it may need to be removed in surgery called lobectomy. Because each lobe of the lung is on its own branch of the respiratory tree, this is easily done without damaging the other lung lobes. Along with chemical therapy, this is the most common treatment for lung cancers that have been diagnosed early.

A sliding table moves the person being scanned into the CT scanning machine.

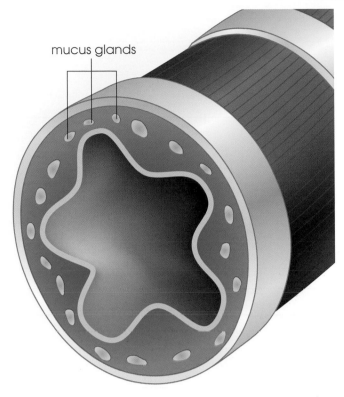

mucus glands

A normal airway is opened wide and not restricted.

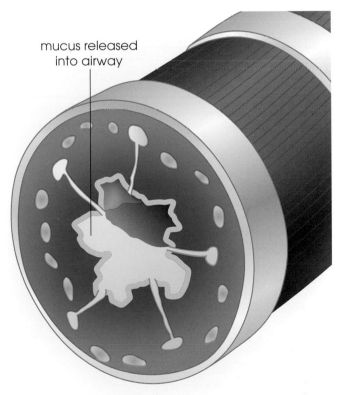

mucus released
into airway

During an asthma attack the airways become
narrowed and mucus is released by the mucus glands.

Asthma

Asthma is a condition which causes episodes of breathlessness. During an asthma attack the bronchioles become narrow, which makes breathing difficult. Asthma also causes increased mucus production, and swelling and inflammation of the airway linings. Children often develop asthma that is caused by an allergic reaction to things such as pollen.

Asthma attacks can be mild or severe and sometimes people need to be hospitalized. Drugs called bronchodilators are used to relieve the symptoms of asthma. They help to open up the narrowed bronchioles.

HEALTH TIP
Using asthma puffers

Many children regularly use puffers or inhalers to treat their asthma. It is important to have this medicine nearby when it is needed. It is also important to only use as instructed by a doctor.

Tip: Follow prescribed doses when using medication.

Taking care of the respiratory system

Basic hygiene and knowledge of first aid procedures, such as **resuscitation**, can be very helpful in taking care of the respiratory system.

Coughs and sneezes

When coughing or sneezing, cover your nose and mouth and turn away, particularly from food. This is an easy and effective way to reduce the spread of respiratory infections. It prevents infectious organisms traveling from one person to another.

HEALTH TIP
Prevent choking
Running around while eating can lead to choking.

Tip: Sit or stand still when eating to help prevent choking.

Choking

It is quite common for people, particularly young children, to choke on food or drink. A simple cough or sneeze can dislodge whatever is blocking the throat. However, if the airways remain blocked, the person may suffocate. Nuts can easily cause choking, as they are small and hard and can easily block air passages.

Sitting down while eating reduces the risk of choking on food and drink.

Resuscitation

Mouth-to-mouth resuscitation and cardio-pulmonary resuscitation (CPR) help the lungs and heart to function if they have stopped. Mouth-to-mouth resuscitation delivers air to the lungs. Cardio-pulmonary resuscitation keeps blood pumping through the body.

In case of emergency

First aid classes teach people how to give mouth-to-mouth resuscitation in an emergency.
First aid courses teach people to:

- clear any blockages from the airways
- lie the patient on their back and tilt the head back slightly
- hold the patient's nose closed and seal their own lips over the patient's lips
- gently blow a breath into the patient's mouth
- move their lips away from the patient's mouth so the air can come out from the patient's lungs

Be prepared

In an emergency you should always seek medical assistance. In the United States emergency services are contacted by dialing 911.

People learn mouth-to-mouth resuscitation at first aid courses.

ACTIVITY Make model lungs

See how resuscitation works when the diaphragm has stopped controlling breathing. You can make a model pair of lungs and simulate mouth-to-mouth rescuscitation using simple items.

You will need

- two balloons
- a plastic bottle with the bottom cut off
- plastic tube
- masking tape
- a three-way hose connector
- poster putty

What to do

1 Cover any sharp edges of the bottomless bottle with masking tape.

2 Connect the tube and the two balloons to the three-way connector.

3 Feed the tube through the neck of the bottle, so that the two balloons hang down inside the bottle.

4 Seal the neck of the bottle with poster putty, to hold the tube in place.

5 Blow into the tube, watching the balloons inflate. The "lungs" will deflate when you take your mouth away from the tube.

Glossary

alveoli	tiny air sacs in the lungs
bronchi	large airways in the chest which branch off from the trachea (a single airway is called a bronchus)
bronchioles	narrow airways in the lungs which branch off from the bronchi and connect to the alveoli
cartilage	strong, bendy tissue in the body
cells	the smallest units of living things
cilia	microscopic hairs on the linings of some airways
diaphragm	a muscle under the lungs which controls breathing
exhalation	breathing out
inhalation	breathing in
lung capacity	the amount of air the lungs can hold
membrane	thin covering on tissues
mucus	lubricating fluid that keeps body structures moist
organisms	living things, including germs and bacteria
pharynx	the respiratory passage in the throat which connects the nasal cavity to the trachea
respiration	the process of gas exchange, where oxygen is taken in and waste gases are taken out
respiratory muscles	muscles in the chest which control breathing
resuscitation	reviving somebody whose heart and lungs have stopped functioning
tissues	groups of similar cells which make up the fabric of body systems
trachea	the airway leading from the throat to the chest

Index